HOW

HISTORY OPENS WINDOWS

The INDUS VALLEY

JANE SHUTER

Heinemann Library
Chicago, Illinois

Designed by Roslyn Broder
Printed and bound in the United States by Lake Book Manufacturing, Inc.

06 05 04 03 02
10 9 8 7 6 5 4 3 2 1

Library of Congress Cataloging-in-Publication Data
Shuter, Jane.
        The Indus Valley / Jane Shuter.
            p. cm. — (History opens windows)
        Summary: An introduction to the civilization of the Indus Valley, which began in ca. 3500 B.C.E., including its culture, government, writing system, and more.
        Inlcudes bibliographical references and index.
        ISBN: 1-4034-0253-1 (HC), 1-4034-0081-4 (Pbk.)
        1. Indus civilization—Juvenile literature. [1. Indus civilization.]
    I. Title. II. Series.
    DS425 .S347 2002
    934—dc21
                                    2002000806

Acknowledgments
The author and publishers are grateful to the following for permission to reproduce copyright material:
pp. 6, 9, 19, 20, 21, 22, 24, 26, 28 H. A. R. P. and Courtesy of the Department of Archaeology and Museums, Pakistan; p. 7 Robert Harding Picture Gallery; p. 8 Borromeo/Art Resource, NY; pp. 10, 11, 15, 16, 25 J. Mark Kenoyer; p. 14 Dilip Mehta/Woodfin Camp & Associates; p. 18 Jehangir Gazdar/Woodfin Camp & Associates, courtesy of the Department of Archeology and Museums, Pakistan; p. 29 Jehangir Gazdar/Woodfin Camp & Associates; p. 30 C. Jarrige

Illustrations: pp. 4, 23 Eileen Mueller Neill; pp. 13, 17, 27 Juvenal "Marty" Martinez
Cover photograph by H. A. R. P. and Courtesy of the Department of Archaeology and Museums, Pakistan

Every effort has been made to contact copyright holders of any material reproduced in this book. Any omissions will be rectified in subsequent printings if notice is given to the publisher.

Some words are shown in bold, **like this.** You can find out what they mean by looking in the glossary.

A note about dates: in this book, dates are followed by the letters B.C.E. (Before the Common Era) or C.E. (Common Era). This is instead of using the older abbreviations B.C. and A.D. The date numbers are the same in both systems.

Contents

Introduction

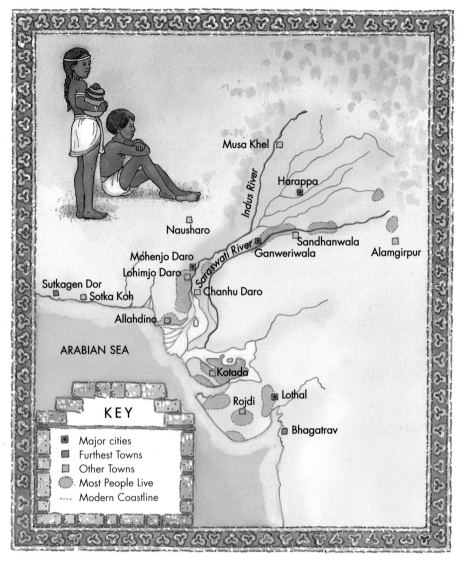

This map shows the Indus Valley civilization. The coastline has changed since those days. You can see both the old and the new coasts on the map.

Musa Khel
Harappa
Indus River
Nausharo
Sandhanwala
Mohenjo Daro
Ganweriwala
Alamgirpur
Lohimjo Daro
Saraswati River
Sutkagen Dor
Chanhu Daro
Sotka Koh
Allahdino
ARABIAN SEA
Kotada
Rojdi
Lothal
Bhagatrav

KEY

- Major cities
- Furthest Towns
- Other Towns
- Most People Live
- ---- Modern Coastline

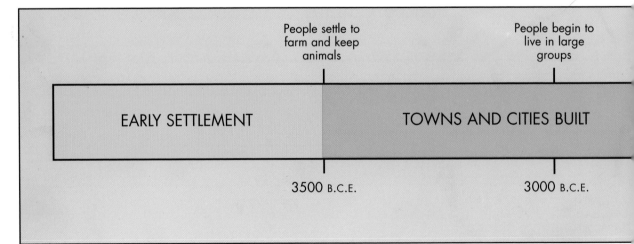

People settle to farm and keep animals

People begin to live in large groups

EARLY SETTLEMENT | TOWNS AND CITIES BUILT

3500 B.C.E.

3000 B.C.E.

The Indus Valley is located in modern Pakistan. People first lived there more than 9,000 years ago. Early hunters settled down to farm the land. People lived in villages, close to the Indus River and the Saraswati River. They began to trade and to live in larger groups.

The Indus Valley civilization began in about 3500 B.C.E. By this time, people lived in cities, where craft workers made beautiful jewelry and decorated pottery. By 2500 B.C.E. there were many towns and villages that were all part of the Indus Valley **civilization.** Because no one has yet **translated** their writing, there are still many mysteries about these people. We do know that after 2000 B.C.E. the cities became less important. The civilization did not suddenly end, but people moved out of the cities and set up smaller settlements in different places.

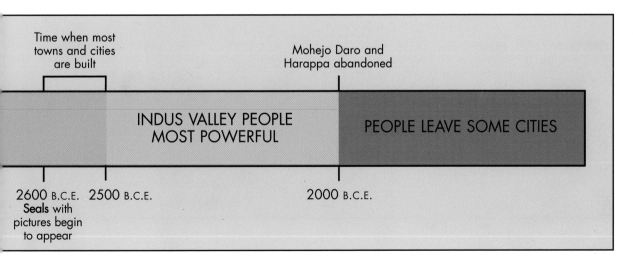

Time when most towns and cities are built

Mohejo Daro and Harappa abandoned

INDUS VALLEY PEOPLE MOST POWERFUL

PEOPLE LEAVE SOME CITIES

2600 B.C.E.
Seals with pictures begin to appear

2500 B.C.E.

2000 B.C.E.

How Was the Indus Valley Ruled?

We do not know exactly how the Indus Valley people were ruled, because we cannot read the writing they have left behind. **Archaeologists** have made guesses about how the **civilization** was run by looking at the remains of the cities.

The Indus Valley cities needed a lot of organizing, so there were probably a lot of **officials** to run things. Archaeologists have made guesses about Indus Valley rulers based on other ancient civilizations that needed the same sort of organization. Most of these civilizations were run by a single ruler, although the Sumerian cities in the Middle East each had their own king. The Indus Valley people were probably ruled in the same way.

Archaeologists think that this carving could be of an Indus Valley ruler.

This board was used for a game that was a little like chess. It tells us that at least some of the Indus Valley people had free time to play games, and that they enjoyed games that involved thinking.

It seems that the Indus Valley people were using the same set of rules all over. Archaeologists have found weights in many towns that all used the same units of weight, similar to pounds and ounces. Bricks for building were also all made to the same size. People were using the same set of rules all over. This usually means that one person or group of people was in charge.

The cities were also very organized. It seems as if there were a lot of officials organizing the cities. Many cities had **drains.** These needed regular cleaning. Some cities may have had a garbage collection system and watchmen on the streets as well. All of this needed people to make sure the work was done.

Religion

We do not know exactly what the Indus Valley people believed. It is clear that water and bathing were important to them, but we do not know if bathing was part of their religious life. We do know that they worshiped nature gods and goddesses. This is very similar to other ancient **civilizations,** where the gods of the Sun, rain, and rivers helped the crops to grow and kept people alive.

Although large buildings have been found the in the Indus Valley cities, there is no building that is clearly a **temple.** People probably had special religious **festivals,** run by priests, when people worshiped together in a holy place. People also prayed at **shrines** in their homes.

This **terra-cotta** statue is probably an Indus Valley goddess. She is most likely a "mother nature" goddess who makes the crops grow every year.

Archaeologists have found a lot of pottery buried in graves. Some is plain and some is decorated. This pottery was found in a grave dating from about 1900 B.C.E.

The Indus Valley people seem to have believed in life after death. They buried people in their best clothes, with things they might need in the afterlife. These included food and drink, stored in decorated pottery containers or baskets lined with waterproof **bitumen**.

People were usually buried lying straight, with their heads pointing north and their feet pointing south. Women wore bracelets on their left arms. The most important people were buried with the best jewelry and the most pots and containers.

Cities

The Indus Valley people built large, walled cities and towns. The two biggest cities were Mohenjo Daro and Harappa. (The Indus Valley people are sometimes called Harappans, after this city.) These two cities covered hundreds of acres, but most others were smaller. Many people, like farmers, lived outside the cities. But it is the cities that show us that they all belonged to one **civilization.**

The cities were built from baked mud bricks that were all the same size. They had a system of **drains,** also built with mud bricks, that ran under the streets. The main streets had wells where people could get water. Many houses had their own wells, too.

The countryside around modern Harappa still looks a lot like it did during ancient times.

Cities were built in two parts. First, there was a "lower town." This was a large walled area full of small houses that were all very similar. Ordinary people lived and worked in the lower town.

The other part of the city was the "upper town." It was built on a high mound of earth, looking down on the lower town and the land around it. It had higher walls and much bigger buildings than the lower town. **Archaeologists** think that this is where the most important people lived. It was probably also where the people who ran the city lived and worked.

Brick drains, like this one at Mohenjo Daro, carried water and waste under the streets to the edge of the city.

Mohenjo Daro

Only part of Mohenjo Daro has been dug up by **archaeologists.** Based on what they have found, they think that about 200,000 people lived in the city when it was at its most powerful.

The upper and lower parts of the city did not join up. They are close together and clearly part of the same city, but there is no sign that there were ever buildings between them. Archaeologists think that a river may have separated the two parts of Mohenjo Daro.

The upper town was built on a platform of mud bricks about 40 feet (12 meters) high. It had several large buildings on it, including the Great Bath. Archaeologists have found the remains of several towers and pieces of wall that suggest that the upper town may have had defenses built around it. Perhaps everyone from the lower town moved to the upper town in times of danger.

This illustration shows the streets of the lower town of Mohenjo Daro.

The buildings in the lower town were smaller than those in the upper town. There were probably homes and workshops for ordinary people.

The streets of Mohenjo Daro were laid out in an almost perfect grid pattern.

A high wall surrounded the upper town.

The side streets run east to west.

The main streets run north to south.

Water

Water was very important to the Harappans. They were the first people to have a system of **drains** and **sewers** in their cities. Many people had bathrooms in their homes, which emptied into a set of drains. Some homes also had their own wells, and there were public wells on the main streets. Everyone could use these.

We do not know why keeping clean was so important. It may have been part of the religion. Also, the Indus Valley people may have understood that it was important for their health to keep clean and to use clean water for cooking and eating.

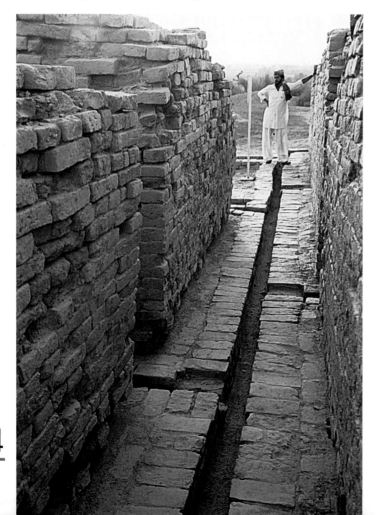

These ancient drains are in a side street in Mohenjo Daro. You can see how the drain in the center of the street is joined by a smaller drain from each house.

The Great Bath at Mohenjo Daro was surrounded by a covered courtyard. There were smaller rooms, some with drains, on one side. Stairs went up to another floor, which would have made this a very grand building.

Mohenjo Daro had a "Great Bath" in the upper town. The pool was waterproof, and it was strong enough to stand the pressure of the water on the bricks when the bath was full.

A brick wall was built with brick supports that pressed inwards. This was covered with a layer of **bitumen** 1.2 inches (3 centimeters) thick. When it dried, it made a waterproof layer. Then the outer brick layer was put down.

The bath and the building around it were very big. It would have taken a lot of work to fill it. Because of this, people think it was probably only used for religious **ceremonies.**

Homes

All houses were built from baked mud bricks. Most homes were at least two stories tall. Some were just two rooms, one on top of the other. But most homes were built around a courtyard, with windows that opened onto the courtyard. Windows had wood or **terra-cotta** bars across them. Roofs were made from mud brick.

Inside, the houses had brick floors. The walls were probably plastered with a thin layer of clay. On the ground floor, there were living rooms and a kitchen. Many houses had a toilet and a washroom that emptied into the main **drain.** The upstairs rooms were probably used for sleeping. They opened onto a balcony over the courtyard.

Archaeologists have found the remains of many Indus Valley homes.

A typical courtyard house probably looked like this.

People probably used the flat roofs to dry laundry. They may have also put up an awning and used them for cooking, sitting, and eating.

People probably did not have much furniture or many possessions.

Houses had doors, but no windows on the outside.

The drains came out from the side of the house to join the street drain.

The doorways to the courtyard allowed air to move around the home.

The homes were built from sun-baked mud bricks.

17

Families

*This beautiful **terra-cotta** cart was probably a child's toy. Several similar carts have been found in Indus Valley towns.*

We do not know exactly how families lived in the Indus Valley. They probably had the same sort of family life as other ancient **civilizations** at the same time. Everyone fit into a "pyramid of power" with a few rulers at the top and a lot of farmers and ordinary workers at the bottom.

Men worked at farming, crafts such as making pots or jewelry, or running the country. They followed their fathers' jobs and taught those jobs to their sons. Women looked after the home and brought up the children. They taught their girls how to raise a family and run a home of their own.

No clothing has yet been found in an Indus Valley city, so we are not sure what the Indus Valley people wore. They grew cotton, so they probably used it to make clothes.

People probably wore different kinds of clothing depending on how important they were. Ordinary people needed loose clothes that were easy to work in. They were not able to buy cloth that cost a lot. They either made their own cloth or bought cheap cloth at the local market.

Rich people wore much finer cotton clothing. It was probably harder to move around in and more richly decorated.

Men and women wore jewelry. These bangles were buried with their owner. Small pots that probably held make-up have also been found.

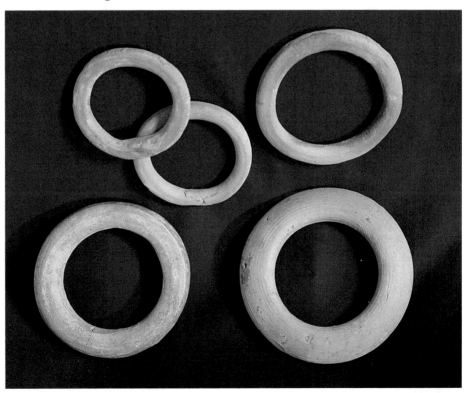

Crafts

Big cities like Mohenjo Daro had many potters, jewelry makers, **bronze** workers, and bead makers. They all lived in different parts of the lower town. Different towns had different craft workers in them, depending on how easy it was to get the things the workers needed. For example, shell bracelets were made in towns close to the coast because shells were easy to find there.

Potters made their pottery on wheels, instead of making each piece by hand from coils of clay. Indus Valley pottery is mostly decorated with complicated shapes. Only a few potters made dishes with people or animals on them. The seal-makers almost always used animals or people in their designs. These **seals** are the first sign of writing in the Indus Valley.

The Harappans made most of their dishes from clay, but bronze pots like this one were often used for cooking.

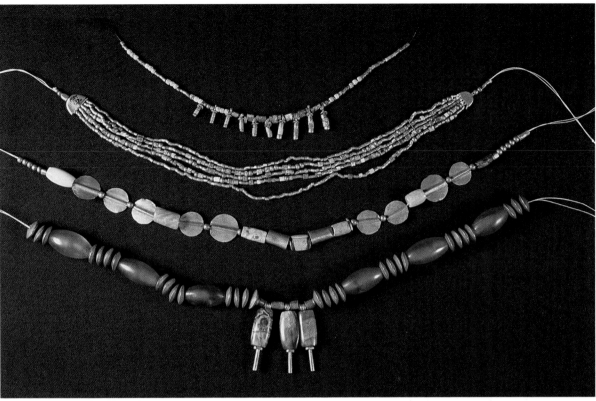

These beautiful necklaces have beads made of gold and stone. The pendant beads on the bottom necklace are held in place by gold wire.

Indus Valley bead makers were especially skilled. The beads were cut and drilled using bronze tools. Some of them were very tiny. The beads were made from gold, silver, precious stones, shells, **terra-cotta,** or a paste of ground-up stone. Working with hard precious stones was especially difficult.

Terra-cotta beads were usually decorated by painting them and heating them in a kiln, in the same way that pottery is glazed. Gold and silver beads and hanging decorations often had patterns carved or pressed into them. Sometimes they had precious stones, too.

21

Trade

The Indus Valley people traded mostly with each other. They traded food and raw materials for making things, as well as **goods** such as pottery and jewelry. Most towns probably had regular markets for the people who lived nearby.

The Indus Valley people also traded with other peoples. They traded food and raw materials, such as gold and wood. We do not know if there was a special group of rich traders, or how far they traveled to trade. They might have moved between just a few trading towns, swapping goods along the way. That way the goods moved over far greater distances than the traders did.

Decorated pottery was often traded along the Indus River.

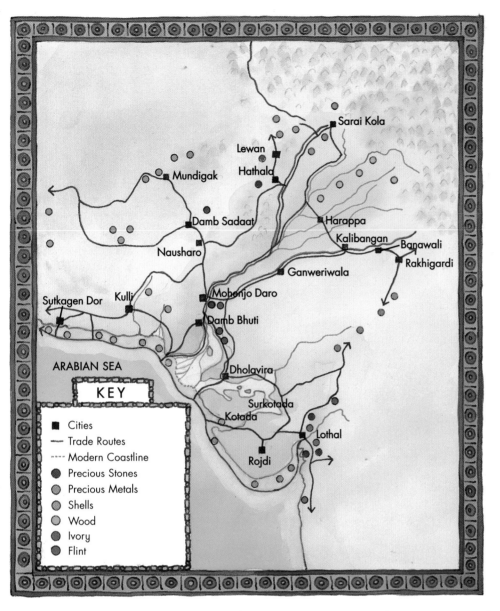

ARABIAN SEA

KEY

- ■ Cities
- — Trade Routes
- --- Modern Coastline
- ● Precious Stones
- ● Precious Metals
- ● Shells
- ○ Wood
- ● Ivory
- ● Flint

Map labels: Sarai Kola, Lewan, Hathala, Mundigak, Damb Sadaat, Harappa, Kalibangan, Banawali, Rakhigardi, Nausharo, Ganweriwala, Sutkagen Dor, Kulli, Mohenjo Daro, Damb Bhuti, Dholavira, Surkotada, Kotada, Lothal, Rojdi

*This map shows the trade routes that **archaeologists** think the Indus Valley people followed, and what they traded.*

Towns that were near the coast often became trading towns, with warehouses for storing all the goods that were traded in and out. The towns of Lothal and Sutkagen Dor were like this. The Harappans also set up towns a long way away from the main area they settled. These towns were useful as places to trade easily with other peoples. They included Shortugui and Shahr-I-Sokhta.

23

Travel

Traders traveled in carts pulled by **bullocks** or by sea in low, narrow boats. Indus Valley boats had a cabin in the middle and were rowed instead of sailed. They do not look as if they were suitable for traveling far out to sea, but they could have traveled up the rivers. They may even have traveled as far as the Persian Gulf or down the western coast of present-day India, if they stayed close to the coast.

Traders would only have been able to travel at certain times. Road travel would have been very difficult in the rainy season. The dirt roads would have become very muddy and hard for heavy carts to travel on.

*This Indus Valley **seal** shows a long, low boat with a cabin in the middle. It is similar to ancient Egyptian boats that traveled the Nile River.*

Ordinary people probably walked where they needed to go, or traveled short distances along the river on small boats. Farmers could have carried things to market on carts pulled by bullocks. It is likely that carts like this might have given lifts to people on market days.

People probably did not need to travel much at all. People who lived in the towns and cities would have been able to walk everywhere they needed to go to. People who lived on farms and in villages would only have needed to travel as far as the nearest town market.

*Even today, carts pulled by bullocks are often used to carry **goods** in parts of the Indus Valley.*

Food and Farming

Indus Valley farmers grew barley and wheat for grain to make porridge, flour, and bread. They also grew beans, chickpeas, and other vegetables.

Farmers kept cattle, water buffalo, sheep, goats, chickens, and pigs on the land that was not good enough for growing crops. Cows, sheep, and goats provided milk and cheese, and chickens were kept for eggs. More than half of all the farm animals were cattle. Owning cows may have shown that you were important. The Indus Valley people were some of the first people that we know kept tame dogs and cats. They may have been used as pets or as work animals.

*The Indus Valley people made tools out of copper, bronze, stone, and bone. This axe head is made of **bronze**.*

*This artist's view shows an Indus Valley family **harvesting** grain.*

The Indus Valley people cooked on **hearths,** either indoors or in the courtyard. Women ground the grain by rubbing a rounded stone across the grains on top of a flat stone. Bread and porridge were an important part of everyone's daily food. Ordinary people mostly ate vegetables and fresh or salted fish. Only rich people ate meat regularly.

27

Writing

The Indus Valley people had a system of writing, but no one has figured out how to read it. Their earliest writing was "picture writing" on **seals.** These seals were probably fixed onto things that were traded. They may have shown who the owner was.

The pictures are usually of animals. Some people have suggested that the Indus Valley people had large family groups that all used the same animal symbol. So you might have lots of families that all used the bull symbol and others who used the unicorn symbol. Other people, however, think the pictures on seals might be religious symbols.

Archaeologists have found pieces of broken pottery with carvings on them. Some of the carvings were made after the piece was broken. They think that the broken pieces of pottery were used as "scrap paper" for writing quick notes.

At first, the Indus Valley people used only pictures on their seals. After a while, they added writing to the pictures. Unlike the case of the ancient Sumerians, no link to help tie the writing to the pictures has yet been found.

We know that the Indus Valley people wrote the first line of writing from left to right, the second from right to left, and so on. So far, 419 different signs have been found. This is too many for them to be a simple alphabet, but not enough for there to be a different sign for every word. So each sign probably makes a sound or a group of sounds that often happen together. Different people have different ideas about what the sounds are and how the language works.

This seal shows a unicorn. More unicorn seals have been found than any other type. People who think the animals show family groups say this might mean people in the unicorn family were important traders.

End of Empire

After 2000 B.C.E., the Indus Valley cities became less important. The **civilization** came to an end at different times in different places. There is no sign that other people attacked the cities. Some cities seem to have become poorer and more crowded before they were deserted.

Mohenjo Daro was badly flooded several times because it was close to the Indus River. Earthquakes in about 2000 B.C.E. may have made the Indus River shift, making it impossible to live in Mohenjo Daro and other cities close to the Indus. At about the same time, the Saraswati seems to have dried up. This could explain why people seem to have moved out of the cities and set up smaller settlements in different places.

This gold cup is from the Quetta culture. These people lived in the Indus Valley after the Harappans.

Glossary

archaeologist person who studies people and objects from the past

bitumen tar-like material used to stick things together

bronze strong metal made by mixing copper and tin

bullock young bull

ceremony set of acts that has religious meaning

civilization the way of life of a group of people

drain pipe or channel that takes water from one place to another

festival time of celebration with special events and entertainment

good something made or grown to trade or swap

harvest season when crops are gathered; or, to gather a crop

hearth area in front of a fireplace

official person who runs a country for the ruler

seal small stone object with pictures or words carved into it. It can be pressed into wet clay to make an impression.

sewer covered drain that carries away water and waste

shrine special place for worshiping gods or dead relatives

temple building for religious worship

terra-cotta baked clay that can be used to make bricks, pots, sculptures, and many other things

translate to put something into another language

More Books to Read

Ali, Daud. *Ancient India.* New York: Anness Publishing, Inc., 2001.

Allard, Denise. *India.* Austin, Tex.: Raintree Steck-Vaughn Publishers, 2000.

Italia, Bob. *India.* Edina, Minn.: Checkerboard Library, 2002.

Index